Flying Across the Ocean:
Yesterday and Today

by Cynthia Swain

Editorial Offices: Glenview, Illinois • Parsippany, New Jersey • New York, New York
Sales Offices: Needham, Massachusetts • Duluth, Georgia • Glenview, Illinois
Coppell, Texas • Ontario, California • Mesa, Arizona

Every effort has been made to secure permission and provide appropriate credit for photographic material. The publisher deeply regrets any omission and pledges to correct errors called to its attention in subsequent editions.

Unless otherwise acknowledged, all photographs are the property of Scott Foresman, a division of Pearson Education.

Photo locators denoted as follows: Top (T), Center (C), Bottom (B), Left (L), Right (R), Background (Bkgd)

Opener ©Bettmann/Corbis; 1 ©Bettmann/Corbis; 3 ©David Butow/Corbis/SABA; 5 ©Hulton Archive/Getty Images; 6 Susan J. Carlson; 8 ©Hulton Archive/Getty Images; 11 ©Hulton-Deutsch Collection/Corbis; 12 ©Bettmann/Corbis; 14 ©Bettmann/Corbis; 16 ©Bettmann/Corbis; 19 ©Bettmann/Corbis; 20 ©Bettmann/Corbis; 22 ©Bettmann/ Corbis

ISBN: 0-328-13586-0

8 9 10 V0G1 14 13 12 11 10 09 08

Today we think nothing of crossing the Atlantic Ocean in just a few hours. We can read, watch a movie, or take a nap while flying. This is much different from the first plane rides. What was air travel across the Atlantic like in the early 1900s? Who made air travel between continents possible?

In 1913, the race to cross the Atlantic by airplane began. In that year, a man named Lord Northcliffe and his newspaper, *The Daily Mail*, offered a huge amount of money to the first person to make a transatlantic flight. However, no plane of the time was capable of such a flight.

World War I (1914–1918) led to many improvements in airplane technology. More powerful engines and better designs allowed planes to carry more weight than ever before over greater distances.

All the same, flying across the Atlantic remained a seemingly impossible obstacle. The ocean was huge—many times wider than any distance that planes had yet flown over water. There was no place, except water, to land in the event of an emergency. The shortest trip across was over the north Atlantic, far from the shipping lanes. The rescue of downed fliers was unlikely in this area.

Lord Northcliffe

The first plane to make the Atlantic crossing was a military plane. On May 16, 1919, three U.S. Navy Curtiss flying boats set off from Newfoundland. They planned to use a series of U.S. destroyers as navigation aids to guide them from Canada to Portugal. A refueling stop was planned in the Azores. The planes were known as flying boats because they could land on water.

The planes ran into two problems: they hit bad weather, and they were separated. Two planes were forced to land at sea. A passing ship rescued one crew. The other crew used the plane's tail assembly as a sail. They rode with the storm for almost three days before reaching land.

The remaining plane, the NC-4, was able to fly on. Fifteen hours and thirteen minutes after leaving Newfoundland, it landed in the Azores. Ten days later, the plane took off again and on May 27 landed near Lisbon, Portugal.

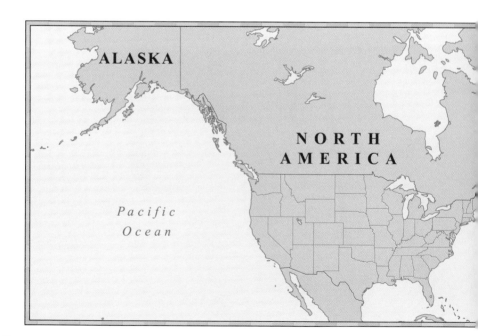

Although the NC-4 was the first plane to make the transatlantic crossing, it did not win Lord Northcliffe's prize. It was completing a military operation.

In the spring of 1919, six planes tried to make the transatlantic flight. One by one, they had problems. Hugo Sundsedt's *Sunrise* crashed during a test flight. Major J.C.P. Wood took off from England with his navigator in the *Shamrock* and headed west toward North America. Barely thirty miles out, the plane's engine died.

In a way, Wood was lucky the engine died so close to land. Given the headwinds that he would have had to fly against—going from east to west—his fuel supply would have run out long before reaching North America. It would be another nine years before a plane completed an east to west crossing of the Atlantic.

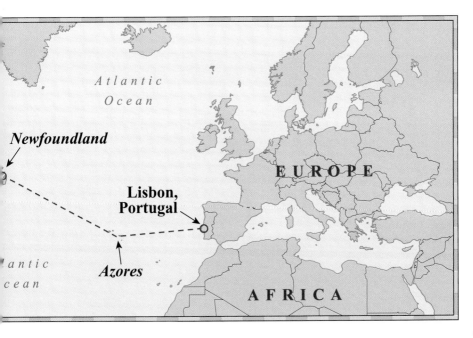

The four remaining planes all planned to start from Newfoundland. The pilots knew that the shortest distance across the Atlantic—about 1,880 miles—was between Newfoundland and Ireland. Also, a tail wind from Newfoundland would help carry them across.

First they had to get their planes to Newfoundland. They shipped the parts. Then they had to find a place to build their planes. There was little level land. They used a horse-drawn roller, heavily weighed down, to flatten out a runway, and built their planes.

Then anxious days and weeks went by as the pilots waited for good weather. On May 18, two planes departed. The *Raymor* crashed on takeoff. The *Atlantic* ran into bad weather and engine problems. Almost halfway across the ocean, its aviators realized they were running out of fuel. In the midst of a storm, they flew to the Atlantic shipping lanes and landed beside a ship. The crew managed to rescue them despite twelve-foot waves.

An early plane, 1919

John Alcock and Arthur Brown were the first to fly from Newfoundland to Ireland, and they did so without stopping. Both men had been in World War I. Alcock had been in the Royal Air Service and Brown had been in the British Army. Both had been prisoners of war. Alcock had planned a flight across the Atlantic while he was a prisoner. Brown had studied navigation.

For their transatlantic flight they chose the Vimy. It was a biplane, meaning it had two sets of wings. It also had a two-man cockpit and a wingspan of about sixty-seven feet. Its two-cylinder Rolls-Royce Eagle Mark VIII engines could generate 360 horsepower each. The Vimy IV **cruised** at about one hundred miles per hour and carried 865 gallons of gasoline.

Alcock and Brown had a lot of problems during their trip. The radio broke soon after they left, so they had no contact with the rest of the world. A little more than three hours after they took off, they ran into fog. They had no idea if they were going the right way.

It was seven hours before they were out of the fog. Then the exhaust pipe on the right engine split. It roared loudly and caught fire. Luckily, the men wore heated flying suits. Then the batteries in the suits ran out, and they nearly froze. The Vimy IV thrashed up and down in gusts of wind. Twice the plane fell to just above the water. When Alcock saw the ocean above his head, he quickly corrected the plane.

John Alcock
and
Arthur Brown

After fifteen hours, they flew into a snowstorm. Ice was a major problem for planes of that **era**. Ice soon covered the engine parts. Snow covered the plane and piled up in the cockpit. Brown climbed out onto the wings and cleared away the snow. He did this four times, while Alcock kept the plane steady. This was not an easy trip, flying blind on a shaky plane.

12

Though the landing of the Vimy IV was rough, both men were fine.

A half hour later, they were flying over Ireland. Even though Alcock spotted a field, they made a rough landing in a swampy bog. Both men climbed out, unhurt. Their trip took sixteen hours and twenty-seven minutes. They won the *Daily Mail* prize and received much praise worldwide. They were even made knights by King George V.

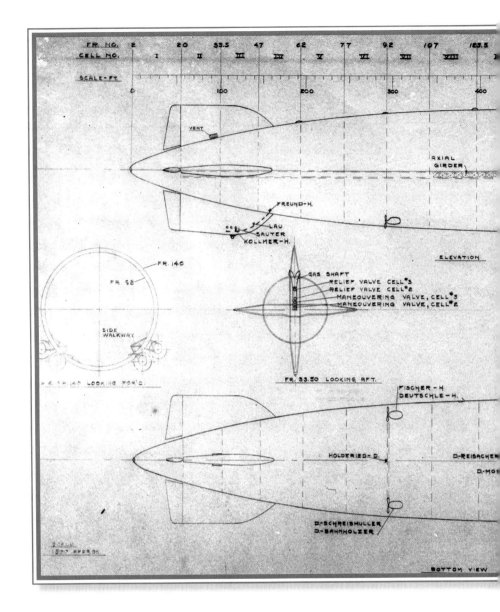

Airships, also called blimps or zeppelins, were different from airplanes and flying boats. They were based on the same basic principles as balloons. A blimp or zeppelin was lighter than air, much slower than an airplane, and could stay in the air longer. A British airship, the *R34*, made the first transatlantic flight by airship when it flew from Scotland to Newfoundland.

14

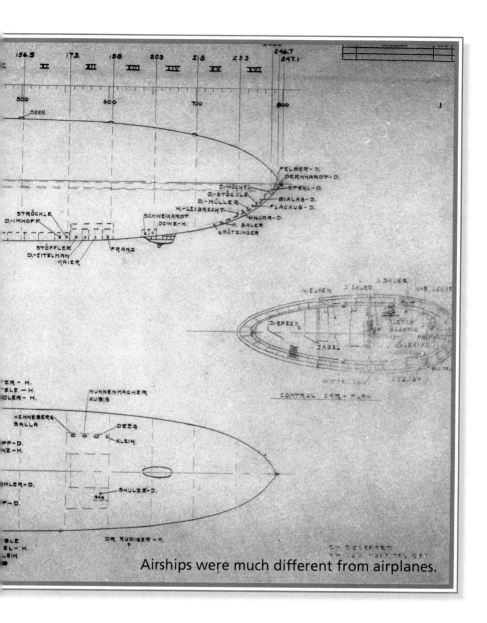

Airships were much different from airplanes.

Airships were larger than any planes of the period. They also offered luxury rooms. The *Graf Zeppelin* had a lounge, a dining area, sleeping cabins, and a complete kitchen. It could carry twenty passengers and more than forty crew members. It made its first flight across the Atlantic when it flew from Germany to New York in October of 1928. In the early 1930s, the airship started the first regular passenger flights across the Atlantic.

The *Hindenburg* was the largest airship ever built. It had space for fifty passengers. There were two decks connected by a wide staircase, and twenty-five staterooms. Each stateroom had its own toilet and hot and cold running water. There was also a dining room with tables covered with white linen and set with fine silver and china, and a lounge with a baby grand piano.

In 1937, the *Hindenburg* took off on an eighty-hour flight from Germany to New Jersey in the

The *Hindenburg*

United States. There were thirty-six passengers and sixty-one crewmembers aboard. It was a smooth flight until a thunderstorm over New Jersey caused a delayed landing. Shortly after the airship dropped its landing lines, it burst into flames.

Twenty-three passengers and thirty-nine crew members survived. A static electricity charge sparked leaking **hydrogen** on fire. The fire caused the **explosion**. The *Hindenburg* event caused the end of airship travel.

One of the most famous long-distance airplane flights happened in 1927. Charles Lindbergh was known as a barnstormer. As a young pilot, he flew from town to town performing stunts in his plane. He got the best flying lessons available by joining the United States Army Air Service. After that, he flew a regular airmail route between St. Louis and Chicago.

Lindbergh was fascinated by the transatlantic challenge. He decided that with the right plane, he could fly nonstop from New York to Paris. Getting the right plane was no easy task, however. Lindbergh could not afford to build or buy a plane on his own.

Charles Lindbergh

People in London cheer Charles Lindbergh as he flies over England on his historic flight.

In May 1919, Raymond Orteig had offered $25,000 to the first pilot to fly without stopping between New York and Paris. Lindbergh believed that this was his chance. Because Lindbergh could not afford a plane, he struggled to get backers. Finally, a company named Ryan Airlines agreed to build his plane.

By 1926, lighter metal began to replace the heavier wood used in aircraft. Planes with one set of wings replaced biplanes. Better air-cooled engines were more reliable and lighter than earlier ones. A much lighter plane saved on gas, allowing a cruising speed of 100 miles per hour. These advancements meant that planes could go farther on a gallon of gas.

Lindbergh's plane was called the *Spirit of St. Louis*. He was very specific about how it was made, and he was known for **criticizing** when even minor errors were made. He insisted on many changes to make the plane better, to make it perfect. Lindbergh was also determined to keep the plane as light as possible.

He knew that his most daring feat was his plan to fly alone. He carefully plotted out the shortest distance between the two cities. At 7:52 A.M. on May 20, 1927, he started off on his heroic journey. Over Canada, rain was **drenching** the plane, but the engine was not affected.

Over the Atlantic, there were problems with bumpy weather and ice. He also had a hard time staying awake, as he couldn't sleep the night before his take-off.

Just before 10:00 P.M. on May 21, Lindbergh saw Paris below him and headed to the airfield. Lindbergh was an instant hero. His humble personality and bravery made him a popular celebrity.

In 1939, Pan American Airways began the first transatlantic passenger service with the *Yankee Clipper*. By then, planes could climb higher to fly above clouds and avoid bumpiness. Jet airliners began passenger service in 1957. Regular transatlantic travel by plane had finally arrived.

Glossary

criticizing *v.* finding fault with.

cruised *v.* flew at the most efficient operating speed.

drenching *v.* wetting thoroughly; soaking with falling liquid, such as rain.

era *n.* a period of time marked by certain events, persons, or things.

explosion *n.* the act of bursting forth with sudden violence or noise from internal energy.

hydrogen *n.* a colorless, odorless, highly flammable gas.

Reader Response

1. Read through the text and find two sentences that are facts and two that are opinions. Use a graphic organizer like the one below to tell how you know fact from opinion.

Sentence	Fact or Opinion?	How I Know

2. Imagine that you could meet Charles Lindbergh. What questions would you ask him about his historic flight? How do you think he might answer them?

3. What clues can you use to help figure out the meaning of *transatlantic* (page 4)? Use the word in a sentence written on a separate piece of paper.

4. Think about the airplanes in this story. What are the differences between these planes and a modern jet?

Suggested levels for Guided Reading, DRA™, Lexile,® and Reading Recovery™ are provided in the Pearson Scott Foresman Leveling Guide.

Social Stud

Genre	Comprehension Skills and Strategy	Text Features
Narrative nonfiction	• Fact and Opinion • Graphic Sources • Ask Questions	• Map • Captions • Diagram

Scott Foresman Reading Street 5.6.4

PEARSON

Scott Foresman

scottforesman.com

ISBN 0-328-13586-0

90000

9 780328 135868

Behind the Motometer

Stories of old cars, singular people and multiple dogs

Robert I. Frey